-1 Thessalonians 5:11

"So encourage each other and give each other strength, just as you are doing now."

Produced and Published by Infinite Generations
137 National Plaza, Suite 300
National Harbor, MD 20745
1-(855)-455-0125
www.infinitegenerations.com

ISBN:
978-1-953364-34-0 (Paperback)

DIVINE ECHOES
OF THE INNER SPIRIT

*Inspirational Words to Encourage
and Uplift your Spirit*

 Infinite Generations Publishing

Acknowledgements

I am thankful to God for the inspirational and motivational quotes put in my spirit by the indwelling of the Holy Ghost. Also, thanks to my mother, Lizzie M. Alston, and my grandmother, Everlena Goode, who taught me the Word of God growing up as a child.

I am also grateful and thankful to others who have made it possible for this book to come forth. Thanks to my daughter, Tiffany, and my two grandchildren, Antonio and Keyauna, for helping with the organization of this book. Thanks to my sons, Clyde, Chad and Lamont for all their support.

Thanks to Infinite Generations Publishers for their generosity and support in helping bring this book forth. The Lord wants His people to have a joyful spirit, therefore, I pray that everyone who reads these quotes will find them encouraging and uplifting.

In loving memory of my daughter Teresa Ann

Introduction

The quotes in this book come through the divine empowerment of the Holy Spirit. As we journey this land and are faced with daily circumstances, 1 Thessalonians 5:11, tells us we are to encourage and uplift one another. You will find many different types of quotes in this book that may apply to your everyday life. There may be several quotes which are just what you need to read at the moment, If so, meditate on that particular quote. Applying God's Word daily is encouraging and uplifting.

The bible addresses many issues on encouraging and uplifting one another. Jesus spoke through stories, songs, poems, miracles, and storms to people who were going through life circumstances. The story in Mark 8:22-26, Jesus heals a blind man. Meditate on what Jesus is saying as you read this quote in the book. Jesus did not ask the blind man, "Can you see?" He asked him, "What do you see?" What an encouraging message He gave to the blind man. Today, the Holy Spirit continues to speak to us just as Jesus did to the blind man during biblical times.

The divine, encouraging, and uplifting quotes in this book are designed to give you spiritual empowerment and strength on how to accept and understand life through different situations.

Table of Contents

Divine Quotes

"There is a big difference between God's eyes and man's eyes. Man can see it, but God can see through it."

"When there is no rain, look for the cloud the size of God's hand."

"The case satan got against you is circumstantial evidence. But the case God got against him is an open and shut case."

"God knows what you are going through, let God fight your battle. After all, He is the heavyweight champion of the world, and He has never lost a fight, and He will never be knocked out."

"The suffering of Jesus Christ was more than physical but personal all the way to the grave."

"*It doesn't take a long-drawn-out prayer to get God's attention. Speak to the Lord in faith as Hannah did, and she received her blessed child from the Lord.*"

"When your arms cannot reach God's arms, God's arms can reach you. After all, can't nobody arm you like God."

"You may be cracked and broken into many pieces, but not beyond God's repair."

"God is in control, and that's how He rolls."

"They nailed Jesus to the cross, and the people said, "If you are the son of God, come down off the cross and save yourself."

Then Jesus looked at me and said, "I'll stay."

Aren't you glad He stayed for you too?

"*Jesus loves me,
this I know, for the nails and
cross tells me so.*"

"Don't give your life to God because He asks you to, but give your life to God because you want to."

"God will never let you go through the valley of the dry bones without a mountaintop experience."

"*Always put God in everything you do because God said, "I am a jealous God, and thy shall have no other god before me.*"

"*God will never give you more than you can bear. Because He bears your heaviest load himself.*"

"*Be a warrior for the Lord because He will give you the power to fight and not be defeated because He knows only the strong survive.*"

"To follow in Jesus' path, you first must follow in His footsteps."

"If you know my story and what I have been through you would say, "Why are you still standing?"

I am still standing because Jesus is the author and the finisher of my story."

"God doesn't have to remind us of our sin. We do a good job of that ourselves."

"Sometimes you must separate yourself from people in order to hear God's voice. God doesn't always speak loudly but in a small still voice."

"*What do you think hurts Jesus the most, the nails or our sins?*"

"God is so powerful that He can destroy the world. Man's sins are so powerful that they can end the world."

"Jesus said, "I went to hell for you. Will you stay out of hell for me?"

"*To give your life to Christ is an honor, and a privilege.*"

"When Jesus opened the blind man's eyes, He didn't ask, "Can you see?"

He asked, "What do you see?" Jesus knew those eyes were going to see, because He will never doubt Himself."

"*Never fear your enemy but let your enemy fear you because we know that fear is the devil, and that is one of the devil's tools.*"

"*Every day that the Lord has made is a blessing. Rejoice and be glad at all times.*"

"God didn't change the way I look, but He changed me from what I was doing. He didn't give me what I wanted, but He gave me what I needed. If he had not, then I wouldn't be here today."

"*When you have a personal encounter with God, you willl never be the same*"

Dianne A. Miller

"*When you can't see God, look to the Son.*"

"A woman with an issue of blood for 12 years was healed by touching the hem of Jesus' garment. Sometimes it's not what you are wearing, but who's wearing it."

"One of the mistakes a person can make is to hold on to things that are worthless, and let go of what is priceless, Jesus"

Encouraging
Quotes

"Sometimes you must release the pressure that is about to destroy you. A Fireman will never run into a burning building without releasing the water to put out the fire."

"*Stop picking out the parts of the Bible that suit you, and start picking out the parts that will grow you.*"

"It is not the size of the person's faith that gets the job done. All it takes is a little faith. David was small in stature, but he had enough faith to defeat a giant. Let your faith overcome your fear."

"How strong is your temper? Can the enemy huff and puff and blow it down?

Or, are you standing on a solid foundation or sinking sand?"

"*A lion doesn't have to show his toughness.*
All he must do is roar to show his authority."

"*When your mind can't think anymore, let your heart take over, and it won't miss a beat.*"

"*If someone asks you for a piece of bread, make them a sandwich because man cannot live by bread alone.*"

"If you want a harvest, you first must plant some seeds. But be careful what seeds you plant because you will reap what you sow."

"One will never be free if one never realizes they are in bondage."

"When your darker days outweigh your brighter days, it will determine how strong you will be able to stand on your worst days."

"*A mistake is not a mistake if you keep doing it. Then it will become a habit.*"

"Men stop lifting up weights and start pulling down strongholds."

"Stop letting people fill your mind with their trash because you are not a trash can or a dumpster."

"Do not let your struggle be the reason why you cannot make it to the top. But let your struggle be the reason why you will stay on top."

"The tortoise never said he could win the race, but he entered the race. He knew that the race was not given to the swift or the strong, but to the one who endures to the end wins."

"When someone won't let you in, don't worry. When one door won't open, God will open a window."

"Stop letting negative people into your space. Because "Bad company ruins good morals."

"*If you live in a glass house, don't throw stones at each other's house. Remember, both houses are made of glass.*"

"Be careful who you hang with because if you hang with wolves, you will run with the pack. Before you know it, you will become one of them, a wolf."

"*If satan can easily steal your joy, then can he easily steal your soul?*"

"Never walk in another man's shoes because you never know where he has been and where he is going. Put on your own shoes because you know where you are going."

"Stop and think before you cut someone with your words. Remember, life and death are in the power of the tongue."

Uplifting Quotes

"You may not be loved for what you are, but you are loved for who God created you to be."

"If you take the time out to count your blessings, then you wouldn't have time to count your problems."

"*If you want to see how strong a small person is, watch them lift up Jesus.*"

"Instead of letting your mountain move your faith, then let your faith move your mountain."

"Be the sunshine in someone's life so they can see in the darkness."

"It takes a carpenter to build a house, but it takes a woman's love to make it a home."

"Don't judge a person for how they look but for who they are."

"As long as you have hate in your heart, love will never show up. The two cannot be mixed."

"The measure of a woman's faith is not how strong she is but how much she believes."

"Only in darkness will the moon show its light. Only in Christ you can see man's light."

"You don't have to have a Ph.D or a master's degree to serve the Lord. All you need is a made-up mind and a willing heart. And that's all it takes."

"God will never give you a battle that you can't win. And He will never put you in a storm He is not in. And He will never take His hands off you."

"To be healed, you first must be sick because Jesus said, "I came for the sick, and not the well."

"There is not one sparrow that falls to the ground that God doesn't see. If He has His eyes on the sparrow, you know He has His eye on you because can't nothing get past those eyes."

"Satan whispered in my ear and said, "I got you, and you are mine."

I whispered back, "You can't touch this."

"When satan knocked me down to the ground, little did he know that I was rooted and grounded in the Lord. And like the grass after the rain, I sprouted back up."

"*Where there's smoke, there's fire, and where there is fire, there is the Holy Ghost, a consuming fire.*"

"It takes a man with faith to walk on water, but it takes a man with doubting faith to drown."

"You may hate me and dislike me, but you will never defeat me."

"Your strength is not measured in how much weight you can lift but in the measure of faith that you have."

"God does not need a towtruck to lift you up. All He needs is just one touch of His finger."

"The only way to be around negative people is to give them a positive jump start in Christ."

Dear Lord, we thank you for your grace and mercy. But most of all we thank you for your Son Jesus Christ because without Him it would be no us. Lord continue to keep and guide us until one day we will all get to see you face-to-face. Amen!

Author's Prayer - Dianne A. Miller

Notes

_____

_____

_____

_____

_____

_____

_____

_____

_____

_____

_____

_____

_____

About the Author

Dianne A. Miller is a Christian Missionary who gave her life to the Lord at a very young age. As a child, she grew up being taught about the Lord by her mother, Lizzie M. Alston, and grandmother, Everlena Goode. They have both gone home to be with the Lord, but she gives them credit for the woman she is today. She honors them by saying, "They are gone but not forgotten."

According to 1 Peter 4:10-11, "Each of you has received a gift to use to serve others. Be good servants of God's various gifts of grace. Anyone who speaks should speak words from God. Anyone who serves should serve with the strength God gives so that in everything God will be praised through Jesus Christ." Dianne is a faithful servant who uses her God-given gifts in various forms to serve others. She participated in her church choir, served on the usher board, and taught Sunday School for over 25 years. Today, she continues working for the Lord as an online Prayer Warrior, a motivational speaker who speaks at jails and prisons or wherever needed. Her missionary work for over 30 years has carried her across many boundaries, such as street ministering, nursing homes, and hospitals.

She is a Counselor at Eckerd Connect Girls Academy, who works with young women between the ages of thirteen and sixteen. A rewarding career she loves. Her Christian knowledge and degree in Criminal Justice enable her to understand how to relate to people from diverse backgrounds. She prays that the counseling they receive will help them to become productive leaders and make a difference in the world. She hopes the quotes in this book will open up a *divine* spiritual intervention, *encourage*, and *uplift* others.

More from the Publisher:
Infinite Generations
Sunday Messages

A faith-based devotional book designed to help you recognize your divine purpose.

Available at
Infinitegenerations.com/shop

Shop at
Infinite Generations
Bookstore Online!

Infinitegenerations.com/shop

Books
Calendars
Magazines
Merchandise
and more!

Available at
Infinitegenerations.com/shop